S0-ABC-602

3.1138 00130 1184

DATE DUE

cool collectibles

TRADING CARDS

Rob Kirkpatrick

HIGH
interest
books

Children's Press
A Division of Grolier Publishing
New York / London / Hong Kong / Sydney
Danbury, Connecticut

To my family

Book Design: Michael DeLisio
Contributing Editor: Jennifer Ceaser
Photo Credits: Cover © The Image Bank; p. 5, 6, 14, 21, 24, 26, 29, 38, © Corbis;
p. 10, 22 © Archive Photos; p. 9, 13, 16, 18, 35, 36 by Dean Galiano; p. 30 by
Thaddeus Harden.

Visit Children's Press on the Internet at:
http://publishing.grolier.com

Library of Congress Cataloging-in-Publication Data

Kirkpatrick, Rob, 1968–
    Trading cards / by Rob Kirkpatrick.
        p. cm.—(Cool collectibles)
    Summary: Surveys the history of trading cards, explains what factors deter-
        mine their value, and describes how to care for and protect them.
    ISBN 0-516-23335-1 (lib. bdg.)—ISBN 0-516-23535-4 (pbk.)
    1. Trading cards—Collectors and collecting—Juvenile literature. [1. Trading
cards—Collectors and collecting.] I. Title. II. Series.

NC1002.C4 K57 2000
741.6—dc21

            99-058249

Copyright © 2000 by Rosen Book Works, Inc.
All rights reserved. Published simultaneously in Canada.
Printed in the United States of America.
1 2 3 4 5 6 7 8 9 10 R 05 04 03 02 01 00

J
769.4
KIR

Contents

NORTHLAKE PUBLIC LIBRARY DIST.
231 NORTH WOLF ROAD
NORTHLAKE, ILLINOIS 60164

INTRODUCTION

Trading cards can be a great item to collect. Trading cards can be a fun hobby, a money-making activity, or both. Some people collect cards because they like to have pictures of their favorite athletes, movie stars, or television characters. Others try to find the most valuable cards and hold onto them. These collectors hope that their cards will increase in value. Trading cards are not just a hobby now. They are a big business.

Most trading cards are 2 ½" by 3 ½" pieces of cardboard. They are sold in packs at your local supermarket or drugstore. At hobby shops, you can buy complete sets of all the cards made by a company that year. You also can buy individual cards at card stores or card shows.

The most popular trading cards are sports cards. Each of these cards has a picture of an athlete on the front. On the back of each card are

Today, baseball trading cards are not just a
hobby, but a moneymaking business.

the player's statistics, such as the number of
touchdowns he scored. Some people collect an
entire set of cards from their favorite sport.
Others collect cards of their favorite players.
Some collectors look for the most valuable
cards. There are many ways to collect.

CARUTHERS, (P. Brooklyn).

OLD JUDGE & GYPSY QUEEN CIGARETTES

THE HISTORY OF TRADING CARDS

The first makers of trading cards were cigarette and tobacco companies. In 1886, Goodwin & Co. produced the first trading cards. They were made of cardboard, with mounted photographs of baseball players, boxers, and other athletes. They were sold inside packets of cigarettes. The cards were very small, measuring just 1.5 by 2 .5 inches (4 cm by 6 cm). These early cards, known as "Old Judges," also were a brand of cigarettes made by the Goodwin company. The company stopped making these cards in 1890. Very few of these cards remain today, so they are extremely valuable. A single Old Judge card can be worth as much as $75,000!

Ballplayer Bob Caruthers "Old Judge" baseball card

CARDS AND CANDY

In the early 1900s, candy companies started producing trading cards. The McCarthy Candy Company was the first to make new sets of cards each year. From 1911 until 1938, they made cards for minor league baseball teams.

The 1920s also saw the creation of other types of trading cards. In addition to baseball cards, Chicago's Exhibit Supply Company produced postcard-size trading cards of actors and actresses.

During World War II (1939–45), there was a paper shortage, so companies stopped making cards. Then in 1948, the Bowman Gum Company began selling baseball cards in packs of gum. Bowman packs cost one cent each and contained one card and one piece of gum. People started to refer to baseball cards as bubble gum cards.

From 1886 to 1935, baseball cards were the most common type of trading card. As collecting caught on, companies began to make trading cards for other sports. In 1935, National Circle

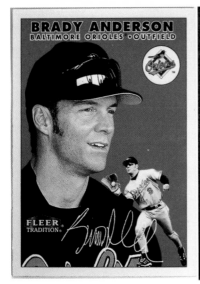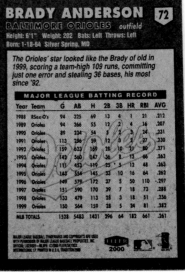

Baseball trading cards are still the most
common type of trading card.

released the first football cards. In 1948,
Bowman Gum began to make basketball cards.
Parkhurst first made hockey cards for the
1951–52 National Hockey League season.

TOPPS ON TOP

In 1951, Topps Chewing Gum produced its first
baseball cards. They made two sets of fifty-two
cards each. One set had cards with blue backs;
the other had cards with red backs. Topps
released a new set every year after that. People
liked the idea of annual (once a year) card sets.

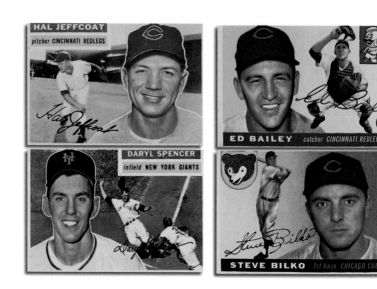

Topps baseball cards started being manufactured in 1951.

Topps made so much money from selling cards that they soon became the only major card producer during this period. The company quickly spread out to include other sports. Topps started releasing hockey cards in 1954, football cards in 1955, and basketball cards in 1957.

For decades, Topps was the only major producer of sports cards. Then in 1981, two new companies, Fleer and Donruss, began producing trading cards. Two other companies, Score and Upper Deck, released sets in the late 1980s. The 1989 Upper Deck baseball set was very popular. These cards were printed on high-stock (good quality) cardboard. The company's 1989 card for Ken Griffey, Jr., is one of the most valuable baseball cards today—worth more than $1,500!

Card collecting reached new heights in the 1990s. Many companies, including Leaf, Pacific, Pinnacle, and Skybox, introduced cards with new features. These included flashy designs and more pictures of and information about players. These recent trends have attracted more people to the hobby. However, some collectors prefer to find cards from the past. They say both the cards and the hobby were once a lot simpler.

A NEW KIND OF COLLECTING

There are collectors who look for nonsport trading cards. These trading cards are made for television shows, movies, musicians, action figures, and even stuffed animals! Comic books such as *Spawn* and *X-Men* have their own trading cards. Starting in the 1970s, trading cards featured characters from popular TV shows and movies, including "Happy Days," "Charlie's Angels," and the *Star Wars* series.

In the 1990s, trading-card games became popular. The card game Magic: the Gathering was one of the most successful. In the Magic game, players collect cards that give them imaginary powers. They build a deck (collection) of powerful cards to use against other players in the game.

Similar card games have been made for TV shows, including "Xena: Warrior Princess." In 1999, the card game Pokémon, based on an animated Japanese TV show, became an enormous hit in the United States.

Fun Fact

In the early days of trading cards, kids used to "flip" cards. As with flipping a coin, when a card hit the ground, the side that it landed on determined who got to keep the card.

Today's trading cards feature characters from popular movies and television shows.

Wheat—Brooklyn Nat.

THE VALUE OF TRADING CARDS

If you've been to a card show or logged onto an online auction, you know that some trading cards are worth a lot of money. Understanding the value of cards can be a confusing business. How can one card be worth fifty dollars while another is selling for just fifty cents?

Many different factors determine how much a card is worth. However, the main question is: How much is someone willing to pay for the card? Price guides and rating systems help collectors to determine how much their cards are worth. However, card collecting is not an exact science. You never can put a specific price on a card. After all, no one ever paid for groceries at the supermarket with a Mickey Mantle baseball card!

Rare cards, such as this one of ballplayer Zack Wheat, are extremely valuable to collectors.

Other popular sports trading cards include
wrestling, basketball, and football cards.

POPULARITY

Trading cards feature athletes from almost every
type of sport. There are auto racing cards, hockey cards, and wrestling cards. The top three
sports in card collecting are baseball, basketball,
and football. The cards featuring the most popular players in these sports usually wind up being

the most valuable. Cards featuring high-profile athletes such as Brett Favre, Grant Hill, Brett Hull, and Mike Piazza are worth more than those of lesser-known players. Cards that picture less-famous athletes are known as commons.

CONDITION

A card's condition is another important factor in determining its value. Because trading cards are made of cardboard, or cardboardlike material, they can be easily damaged. Many collectors like to have cards that are practically new. These are cards that are in mint (perfect) condition. The closer to mint a card is, the more valuable it is.

ROOKIE CARDS

In general, cards that are hard to find will have a higher value. For this reason, the very first cards made of an athlete are often the most valuable. These cards usually are produced during the player's rookie (first) year as a professional athlete. Often, the cards are made before the athlete has proven his or her skills as a player. If the athlete becomes a star, there will be a high demand for his or her rookie card. That player's minor league cards will be worth more, too.

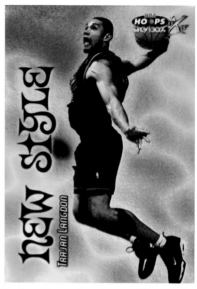

Trajan Langdon's rookie card

CARD RUNS

A card run is the number of copies of a card that a company produces. The easier a card is to obtain, the less money it will be worth. For example, each year Topps makes several thousand copies of each player's card. It means that the chances of opening up a pack and finding a certain player's card are high. Also, because Topps produces so many cards, the company can sell them at a low cost. A pack of eleven Topps cards costs less than two dollars.

In comparison, many smaller companies make packs that contain only five cards. These packs can cost more than five dollars. The card runs are shorter, which means there are fewer available copies of a player's card. Because these cards are harder to get, they are more valuable.

INSERT CARDS

Insert cards (also called inserts) are some of the most valuable cards in today's market. Inserts are included in complete sets or in random packs sold in stores. Inserts are much harder to find than are regular issue cards. For example, the odds are that you would have to buy eight packs of Press Pass '99 Basketball cards before finding a special autographed insert. If you are looking for a 1996 Upper Deck Football "Game Jersey" insert card, the odds are that you would have to buy 2,400 packs before you find one!

Because insert cards are harder to find, they usually are worth more money. They also are more valuable because they have special features that regular cards do not. Inserts have some of the flashiest designs and newest pictures of players. Sometimes inserts have extra statistical information about players. Players sometimes sign their cards before the cards are put into packs. Some inserts, called die-cuts, are cut in odd shapes instead of the usual rectangle. (For example, one insert set of baseball cards was in the shape of a baseball glove.) Some inserts may even have pieces of the player's jersey sewn onto the card! Some collectors feel that the insert trend has added an exciting new dimension to card collecting. Others feel that these inserts have cheapened the hobby.

AUTOGRAPHS

Collectors love to have cards of their favorite players. It is an even bigger thrill if they get their

Mark McGwire signs autographs after a
St. Louis Cardinals game.

favorite player's autograph on a card! You often
can find players signing cards at sporting events
and card shows. Some collectors will even mail
a player his or her own card to sign. In this case,
you should send a self-addressed, stamped enve-
lope with the card. The card you send should
not be an especially valuable one. There is no
guarantee that the player will send it back.

Topps produces new sets of cards each year.

SET VALUE

Most trading card companies produce new sets each year. These sets contain cards for most or all of the players in a particular sport.

It's hard to say what makes one set more valuable than another. If a set has a lot of cards featuring rookie players, it may be more popular with some collectors. Other collectors prefer a particular brand's design or photography. As a collector, you may want to decide which brand you like the most. Buy a few sample packs to see which brand (or brands) you prefer before you spend the money on a whole set.

BUYING TRADING CARDS

More than a century has passed since trading cards were first sold in cigarette packs. Cards also are no longer sold with sticks of gum. Collectors complained that the gum stained the cards. Today, trading cards can be purchased and sold in a number of different ways.

BUYING PACKS

One way to purchase cards is to buy individual packs. Each pack contains anywhere from one to twelve cards, depending on the brand. However, many collectors think that buying packs is not the best way to collect cards. Collectors argue that you can't be sure which cards you are getting in any given pack. You might get your favorite player in the first pack

WEEN THE ACTS & BRAVO
CIGARETTES

ETELKA GERSTER.

PEDRLINER & MAURER, 22 & 24 N WM ST. N.Y.

BETWEEN THE ACTS & BRAVO
CIGARETTES

EVA BARRINGTON.

LITH. BY F. HEPPENHEIMER'S SONS. 22 & 24 N WM ST. N.Y.

BETWEEN THE
CIGARE

MISS BAR
in ZOZO as the MA

LITH. OF HEPPENHEIMER & MAURER.

EEN THE ACTS & BRAVO
IGARETTES

BETWEEN THE ACTS & BRAVO
CIGARETTES

BETWEEN THE
CIGARE

you buy. Or you might have to buy fifty packs before you find that card. This can be a very costly process. It also can take a lot of time. On the other hand, some collectors enjoy the thrill of opening up a pack to see which cards they have just purchased.

BUYING SETS

If you do not want to collect cards by individual packs, you may want to purchase a complete set. For instance, Upper Deck made a set of 255 different player cards in 1999. This set is valued at around $30. If you purchase a complete set, you get one card of every player. The drawback is that you have to pay more money for a set than you would if you bought the packs separately. Also, many collectors feel that you lose out on the thrill of collecting when you buy complete sets. One of the advantages of buying sets is that you usually get one or more special insert cards.

Trading cards haven't been sold in cigarette packs for more than one hundred years.

Hobby shops are one place to find trading cards.

WHERE TO BUY CARDS

In the past, trading cards often were difficult to locate. Today, it's easier than ever to try to find the card you're seeking. Now there are many places where trading cards are bought and sold.

Stores

Trading cards can be bought in supermarkets and drugstores. You also can buy them in special hobby shops or comic book stores. Check your local Yellow Pages for listings under Hobby, Cards, or Comic Books.

Advertisements

In most trading-card magazines, there are advertisements for buying cards through the mail. Companies will sell you complete sets, boxes of card packs, individual cards, and autographed cards. To order from these companies, you will have to send a check or money order in the mail.

You also can order over the phone with a credit card. However, there's no guaranteeing in what condition these cards will be. Some collectors may only want to buy cards if they can see them first.

If you buy a card through the mail, be sure the company is sending you the card you want. Check to see whether the card is in the same condition in which it was advertised to be. If it is not, contact the company and ask for your money back.

Card Shows

Check your local newspaper for card shows coming to your area. Visiting these shows can be fun whether or not you buy any cards. You will get to see a wide selection of trading cards from both past and present. Card shows are a good way to meet people who have a similar interest. You also will be able to see a card and check its condition before you buy it.

Internet

You might also be able to find the card you want at an online auction. An auction is a public sale where things are sold to people who make the highest bids. A bid is when you say how much you will pay for something.

If you have access to the Internet, you can go to an auction Web site, such as Amazon.com, eBay, or Beckett Collectibles Online. You can do a search for the athlete and get a list of cards that are being auctioned. If you want one of

ARE YOU LOOKING TO BUY OR SELL VINTAGE SPORT CARDS?

NetTRADE
Sportscard Auctions

Your site on the Net where you can find all your card collectibles

The NetTrade line-up of internet/telephone auctions gives you more ways to buy more and better sports cards. Now you can fill out your own line-up with Certified Sports Cards.

Your can bid by touchtone phone or at our website. Bid as often as you like on the cards you like. You decide how much your want to pay. So you never pay more than you want to.

Get in on NetTrade specials. Call toll-free for your confidential bidder's identification number. There is no charge to register. And we back your purchases with a no-questions-asked return policy.

For solid VALUE at unbeatable prices, visit the website where the experts go.

Get your Cards today.

Register Today www.nettrade.com or 1-800-555-5555

NetTRADE
Sportscard Auctions

A subsidiary of MaryJaneAuctions, Inc.

29 East 21st. Street • New York, New York 10017 • (Tel) 212-555-5555 • (Fax) 212-555-5555

An example of an advertisement you might see in a trading card magazine.

these cards, you can place a bid, which is the highest amount of money you are willing to spend on the card. If someone else places a higher bid, you can decide to raise your bid, or you can let the other bidder win the card.

It can be fun and exciting to place bids, but you always should be careful not to bid more than you want to spend. Remember, if you "win" a card at an auction, you still have to pay money

29

for it. You will have to send a check or money order in the mail to the seller. Then the seller sends you the card you won at the auction.

Trading

Of course, you do not always have to pay money for cards. You may be able to trade for them with another collector. They are called trading cards, after all. For decades, collectors have traded cards with one another. You may

want to consider trading a card if:

- You have cards of players that you are not collecting.
- You have an extra (double) of a player whose card you collect.

You might be able to trade the card to someone else in exchange for the card or cards that you want.

PRICE GUIDES

With all of these options for buying cards, it's important to be a smart collector. Educate yourself about the hobby. Before you spend money on cards, you should buy a price guide. Price guide magazines, such as *Beckett Sports Collectibles and Autographs* and *Tuff Stuff*, are published each month. These magazines help you to understand the value of different cards. In each magazine, there is a list of all the sets of cards that the major brands have made in the past. Next to each listing of a set or individual

You can use the Internet to participate in online auctions of trading cards.

cards, there is a listing of that set or card's value to collectors. The listings help collectors to figure out how much they should expect to pay for cards at stores or shows. Trading-card magazines also include stories on trends in the hobby. The Beckett company publishes separate monthly magazines for baseball cards, basketball cards, football cards, hockey cards, Pokémon cards, and sports autographs.

Fun Fact

One trading card price guide lists these cards as being the most valuable in each sport.

Baseball: 1909 "T206" Honus Wagner	$225,000
Basketball: 1948 Bowman George Mikan	$9,000
Football: 1935 National Circle Bronko Nagurski	$7,500

4

BUYING SMARTLY AND SAFELY

While card collecting may be an enjoyable hobby for some, for others it's big business. As with any business, collectors should be careful before they spend too much money. Be aware of these situations before you buy:

- Card stores need to make a profit from what they sell. Sometimes a store may overcharge for its merchandise. If you think a card is too expensive at one shop, check around to see if you can get it for less somewhere else.
- Television shopping networks often are not good places to buy cards. They sell cards to home shoppers at a high profit. Often, these shoppers are impulse buyers, which means they buy something quickly without giving much thought to the price.

NORTHLAKE PUBLIC LIBRARY DIST.
231 NORTH WOLF ROAD
NORTHLAKE, ILLINOIS 60164

- Supermarkets may charge a lot of money for "special" packages of cards. These packages may contain only cards of no-name players.
- Be careful when you purchase cards through magazine ads. Unlike buying cards at a store or show, you do not get to see the actual cards before you buy them. Look for ads with companies that promise a money-back guarantee. You may not want to respond to ads placed by an individual. The magazines that publish these classified ads are not responsible if the advertiser cheats you out of merchandise.
- At online auctions, be careful about which cards you bid on. Even if the seller includes pictures of the cards, you should check to see if the person previously has sold cards on that Web site. For example, the eBay site shows comments from both bidders and sellers. This feature lets people know which buyers and sellers have made honest deals and which ones are not reliable.

Magazines about collectible cards can help you to
know how much to spend on certain cards.

LET THE COLLECTOR BEWARE

It's important to watch out for counterfeit cards.
A counterfeit card is a fake card that looks like
one made by a real card company. Counterfeiters
make fake cards and sell them to collectors.
Usually, counterfeiters choose the most valuable
cards and make fake copies of them.

Most likely, a card selling for $3 at your local
comic book store is not a fake. But if you are looking to invest a lot of money in this hobby, then
you should be sure of what you are buying.

Price guides report on which cards are likely
to have counterfeits. To be safe, look for cards that

Mint (MT)–A card with four sharp corners. 50/50 centering, no imperfections or signs of wear. Many cards right out of the pack do not greade mint. Pre-1970 MT cards typically sell at 150% or more of the NM price.

Near Mint (MT)–A near perfect card with perhaps one minor imperfection. Centering is no worse than 60/0 and the card must have original gloss. NM cards are the standard by which other grades are usually gauged.

Excellent Mint (EX-MT)–A card with only two or three minor imperfections. Must have original gloss and centering no worse than 70/30. EX-MT cards typically sell for 75%-90% of the NM price.

Excellent (EX)–A card with a few minor emperfections. Some original gloss is lost and the edges show moderate wear. All four corners typically show some wear. Centering is no worse than 75/25. EX cards usually sell for 50-75% of the NM price.

Very Good (VG)–A card that shows obvious handling but is still attractive despite wear and imperfections. A VG card may have a crease, but should not be severe enough to make the card unattractive. Most of the original gloss is lost. VG cards usually sell for 25%-35% of NM price.

Good (G), Fair (F), Poor (P)–A very worn card with many major imperfections. Cards of these grades are used as fillers until better ones can be found. With little market for such cards, they are valued at 5%-10% of the NM price.

Minor Imperfections: slightly worn corners, frayed edges, printing marks and light surface scratches. **Major Imperfections:** severe corner wear, wax stains, rubber band mars, sun dading, misuts, creased, tape, stains, thumtack holes, writing, and heavy scratches.

A grading system will help you to identify
the condition of your card.

have been authenticated by a professional grading service, such as the Beckett Grading Service (BGS). (You can find the BGS at *www.beckett.com*.) For a fee, these companies will give your card a number grade between one and ten. A grade of ten means your card is in mint condition. It may be easier to trade or sell a card once you have had it graded. A graded card gives other collectors an objective opinion on the condition of your card.

A REAL AUTOGRAPH?

Autographed cards are often the ones most in demand because they are so valuable. Unfortunately, players' signatures can be forged (faked). Unless you are a handwriting expert, you cannot be certain that an autograph is real. Sometimes, signed cards come with certificates of authenticity (COAs). A certificate of authenticity guarantees that the real player has signed the card. However, these certificates also can be faked. If you are an autograph seeker, the only sure method is to get the signatures yourself.

Fun Fact

There are companies that will make you your own personal trading card. You can send a photo of yourself playing your favorite sport. Then they make a card for you that will make you look like you're a real pro.

5

MAKING THE MOST OF YOUR HOBBY

Once you find a trading card you like, you'll want to keep it in good condition. Your little brother, the family dog, and even the oil on your fingertips can damage the condition of your prized cards. It is a good idea not to expose your cards to direct sunlight or humidity (moisture). These conditions could cause cards to fade or warp (bend). There are several ways to keep your collection in the best possible condition.

PROTECTING YOUR CARDS

The days of collectors keeping cards in shoeboxes is long gone. Most collectors like to keep their cards in some sort of protective covering. Soft plastic "top loading" slips are a popular item. They protect cards from scratches and

You can preserve valuable cards, such as this 1909 Honus Wagner (Pittsburg) card, in plastic.

prevent oils on your skin from rubbing off on the cards. These soft slips often are used together with harder plastic frames. The frames keep the cards from getting creased.

Collectors may choose to keep their cards in plastic sheets. These sheets usually hold nine cards each. They come with three holes in the margin so that they can be kept in binders. Some card stores sell special binders for card collecting. But you also can use binders like those you use for notebooks in school.

Sometimes, collectors want to display their favorite card on a desk or table. You can buy a special frame that holds cards. There also are wall-mounted cases that you can buy to display your cards.

SELLING YOUR CARDS

As they build their collections, some collectors may plan to sell their cards in the future. Collectors who want to sell their cards can do so at a number of places. They can sell them at card shows, hobby stores, or in online auctions. However, because many people are looking for bargains, don't expect to make a huge profit when you sell your cards.

HAVE FUN!

Remember that the main reason to collect is for fun. Here are some tips to help make your card collecting experience enjoyable:

- **Collect the cards you enjoy and in which you are interested.** Don't try to collect from all the trading cards available.
- **Collect for fun, not for profit.** Although you may someday be able to make a profit on the cards you buy now, the true value of trading cards is in the enjoyment they bring.
- **Take it slowly.** Part of the fun of collecting trading cards is browsing through the many types of cards. Enjoy your search! Take the time to discover new and exciting cards.

New Words

annual happening every year

auction a place where items are bought and sold

bubble gum card a type of card sold in a pack of bubble gum

card run the number of copies of a card that a company produces

certificate of authenticity (COA) a document which proves that something is not fake

common a card that features a less-famous athlete

complete set a collection of every card in a series from a given year

condition the physical state of an object

counterfeit fake

die-cut an insert card that has been cut into an odd shape

double more than one of the same card

exchange a trade of one thing for another

forged made to look real; faked

grading putting a value on a card based on its condition

hobby an activity you do for fun in your spare time

humidity moisture in the air

insert card a rare or special card randomly placed in a pack of regular cards

minor league a group of baseball teams made up of players who are trying to make it into the major leagues

Old Judge a type of trading card that was sold in a pack of cigarettes

pack a way that cards are sold; there can be anywhere from one to twelve cards in a pack

price guide a publication that gives the buying and selling prices of cards

profit money that is made by selling goods

rookie a player in his or her first year

set a series of cards that contain most or all of the players in a particular sport

statistics information about a player

For Further Reading

Beckett, James. *Baseball Cards 2000*. New York: Ballantine Books, Inc., 1999.

Larson, Mark K., Editor. *Getting Started in Card Collecting*. Wisconsin: Krause Publications, 1993.

Myotis, Gille and Alexander Gekko. *The Pokémon Edition of Swap: Create Your Own Trading Cards*. Washington: Pride Publications, 1999.

Owens, Thomas S. and Diana S. Helmer. *Inside Collectible Card Games*. Connecticut: Millbrook Press, 1996.

Resources

eBay Auction

www.ebay.com

This site features online auctions of a wide selection of products, including collectibles. You can post as well as bid on current auctions. Use the eBay library to learn more about different types of collectibles.

Fleer/Skybox

1120 Route 73
CSC Plaza, Suite 300
Mt. Laurel, NJ 08054

http://fleerskybox.com

This site features a large collection of articles about Fleer and Skybox products and includes information about current card sets. There also is promotional information about upcoming events.

NonSport Card Collector

http://24.3.47.19/nscc/

This Ezine on nonsport trading cards gives information and industry news on trading cards that are unrelated to sports. The photo gallery has images of past and present products. The site sponsors a collector's forum, where collectors can chat. It also features contests and prizes.

Topps

401 York Avenue

Duryea, PA 18642

www.topps.com

The Topps site contains detailed articles on new products. You can view samples of sports cards, play a trivia game, and read about the history of the Topps company.

Index

About the Author

Rob Kirkpatrick is an editor and freelance writer in New York City. He got his first pack of Topps baseball cards in 1974.